MW00884939

THIS BOOK
BELONGS TO:

_____

_____

Copyright©2022

All rights reserved. No part of this
publication may be reproduced, distributed,
or transmitted
in any form or by any means, including
photocopying, recording,or other electronic
or mechanical methods, without the prior
or written permission of the publisher

I AM 6 & HAPPY

I AM 6 & I CAN MAKE A DIFFERENCE

Thank you for
purchasing
This book .if you
enjoyed
The feedback on
amazon
Would be greatly
appreciated .

Made in the USA
Monee, IL
24 January 2023

26149905R10083